Colors of Imagination:
A Journey Through Art

Isachioaia Vlad

Copyright © 2024 Isachioaia Vlad

ISBN :9798338273142

All rights reserved.

CONTENTS

Acknowledgments
Dedication

1	**Fragmented Reality**	1
2	**Elegant Contemplation**	3
3	**Ethereal Reverie**	5
4	**Veil of Dreams**	7
5	**Keys to the Soul**	8
6	**Embrace Behind Bars**	10
7	**Harmony of Life and Death**	11
8	**Dance of Light and Shadow**	14
9	**Essence of Strength**	15
10	**Embrace of Unity**	17
11	**Whispers of Emotion**	18

Acknowledgments

I extend my heartfelt gratitude to Jiji Madalina for her incredible artistry and generosity in allowing me to showcase her work in this book. Your stunning creations have not only inspired me but have also brought a unique perspective to the world of art. Each piece reflects your dedication and passion, and I am honored to share them with a wider audience.

Thank you, Jiji, for trusting me with your art and for the opportunity to celebrate your journey as an artist. Your talent and vision shine through every image, and I am deeply appreciative of the chance to bring your remarkable stories to life within these pages. This book is a testament to your creativity, and I hope it resonates with all who encounter it.

DEDICATION

To Jiji Madalina, an artist whose vision knows no bounds. Your creativity shines through every stroke of your brush, transforming simple moments into extraordinary expressions of emotion. Your ability to capture the essence of life inspires those around you, reminding us all of the beauty in the world.

This dedication is a celebration of your passion and dedication to the art you create. You have a unique gift for connecting with others through your work, inviting viewers to see the world from your perspective. Each piece tells a story, reflecting your journey and the experiences that shape your artistic voice.

Your art is a beacon of hope and expression, reminding us that creativity has the power to heal and unite. Each canvas you touch becomes a portal to a world where emotions dance freely, inviting us to explore our own feelings. Thank you for your unwavering spirit and for encouraging us all to embrace our artistic journeys with open hearts. Your dedication to your craft is a gift to the world.

1|FRAGMENTED REALITY

This artwork presents a striking juxtaposition of a serene landscape and a fragmented portrait. The upper section depicts a tranquil sunset with soft clouds hovering over distant mountains, evoking a sense of peace and tranquility. The warm hues of the sky blend seamlessly with the gentle contours of the mountains, creating a harmonious backdrop that invites viewers to lose themselves in the beauty of nature. In stark contrast, the lower section of the painting features an abstract, deconstructed face rendered in shades of blue and white. The face appears to be peeling away from the canvas, with fragments floating in the surrounding space. This visual dichotomy may represent the complexity of human emotion and perception, suggesting that beneath the calm exterior lies a world of inner

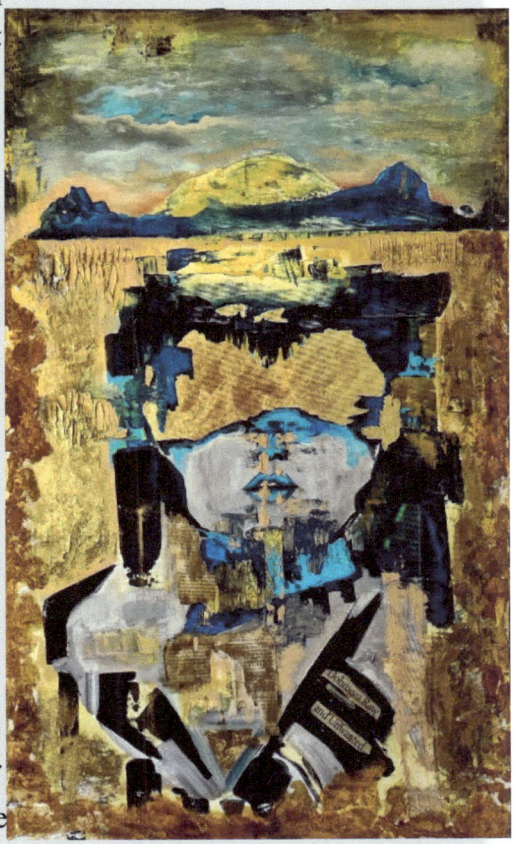

turmoil and fragmented thoughts.

The use of texture and color depth adds to the painting's compelling allure. The artist's technique of layering paint creates a tactile quality that draws viewers in, encouraging them to explore the intricate details of the composition. The contrast between the smooth, serene landscape and the rough, fragmented portrait highlights the tension between external appearances and internal realities.

This artwork invites viewers to reflect on the duality of existence and the multifaceted nature of human experience. It challenges us to consider how we present ourselves to the world versus what we feel inside. The painting's rich symbolism and emotional depth make it a captivating piece that resonates on multiple levels, offering a profound commentary on the human condition.

The serene landscape in the upper section, with its soft clouds and distant mountains, symbolizes the outer calm and beauty that we often project to the world. The warm, inviting colors evoke a sense of comfort and peace, suggesting a desire for harmony and balance in our lives. This part of the painting can be seen as a metaphor for the idealized version of reality that we strive to maintain.

In contrast, the fragmented portrait in the lower section represents the inner chaos and complexity of human emotions. The deconstructed face, with its peeling fragments, suggests a sense of vulnerability and disintegration. The use of blue and white tones adds a cold, almost clinical feel to this part of the painting, emphasizing the stark difference between the outer and inner worlds. Overall, "Fragmented Reality" is a powerful and thought-provoking piece that challenges viewers to reflect on the duality of their existence. It highlights the tension between the serene, idealized exterior and the chaotic, fragmented interior, offering a profound commentary on the human condition. The painting's rich symbolism, emotional depth, and compelling visual contrast make it a captivating and memorable work of art.

2|
ELEGANT CONTEMPLATION

This painting features a striking figure with an elegant, exaggerated hairstyle and bold red lips. The figure's eyes are closed, suggesting a moment of deep thought or calm introspection. The serene expression on the face conveys a sense of peace and tranquility, inviting viewers to ponder what thoughts or dreams might be occupying the subject's mind.

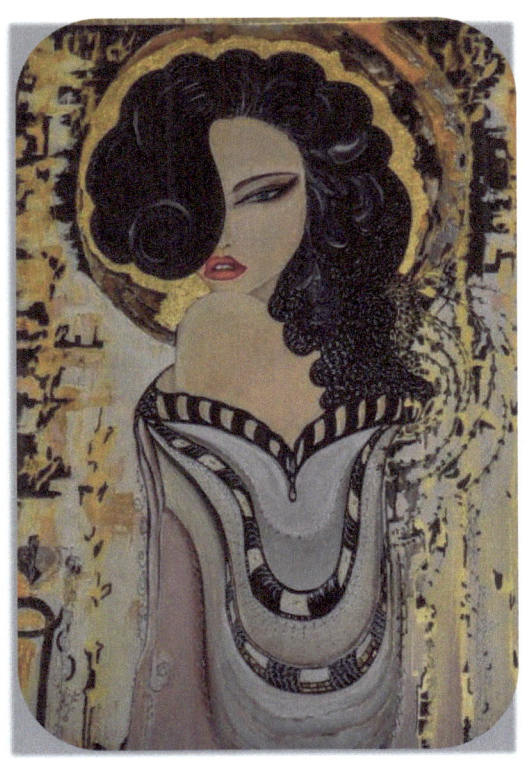

The background is abstract, with splashes of gold and neutral tones that create a dynamic contrast with the figure's pale skin and dark hair. These abstract elements add depth and complexity to the composition, drawing the viewer's eye across the canvas and encouraging a deeper exploration of the artwork. The use of gold hints at a sense of luxury and timelessness, while the neutral tones provide a balanced backdrop that enhances the figure's striking features.

The blend of realistic portraiture and abstract art in this piece creates a unique and intriguing visual experience. The detailed rendering of the figure's features, such as the delicate eyelashes and the subtle shading around the eyes, showcases the artist's skill and attention to detail. Meanwhile, the abstract background elements add a layer of mystery and invite viewers to interpret the scene in their own way.

The figure's hairstyle, with its intricate and exaggerated design, adds an element of sophistication and elegance to the painting. It contrasts beautifully with the simplicity of the closed eyes and the calm expression, creating a balance between complexity and serenity. The bold red lips serve as a focal point, drawing attention to the face and adding a touch of drama to the composition.

"Elegant Contemplation" is a captivating artwork that combines beauty and introspection. It invites viewers to pause and reflect, to consider the inner world of the subject, and to appreciate the harmonious interplay between realism and abstraction. This piece stands out not only for its aesthetic appeal but also for its ability to evoke a sense of calm and contemplation in those who view it.

The painting's rich textures and vibrant colors make it a visually engaging piece that captures the viewer's attention. The contrast between the smooth, polished look of the figure and the rough, textured background adds to the overall impact of the artwork.

In essence, "Elegant Contemplation" is more than just a visual treat; it is an invitation to explore the depths of human emotion and thought. It encourages viewers to look beyond the surface and to find meaning in the subtle details and contrasts within the artwork. This painting is a testament to the artist's ability to blend technical skill with emotional depth, creating a piece that resonates on multiple levels.

3| Ethereal Reverie

This painting captures a dreamlike scene where reality and imagination intertwine. The central figure, with closed eyes and a serene expression, appears lost in a moment of peaceful introspection. The elegant hairstyle and bold red lips add a touch of sophistication, creating a striking focal point that draws the viewer's attention. The figure's calm demeanor invites us to ponder the thoughts and dreams that might be occupying their mind, offering a glimpse into a world of inner tranquility.

The abstract background, with its splashes of gold and neutral tones, adds depth and complexity to the composition. These elements create a sense of timelessness and mystery, contrasting beautifully with the detailed portrayal of the figure. The use of gold hints at luxury and opulence, while the neutral tones provide a balanced backdrop that

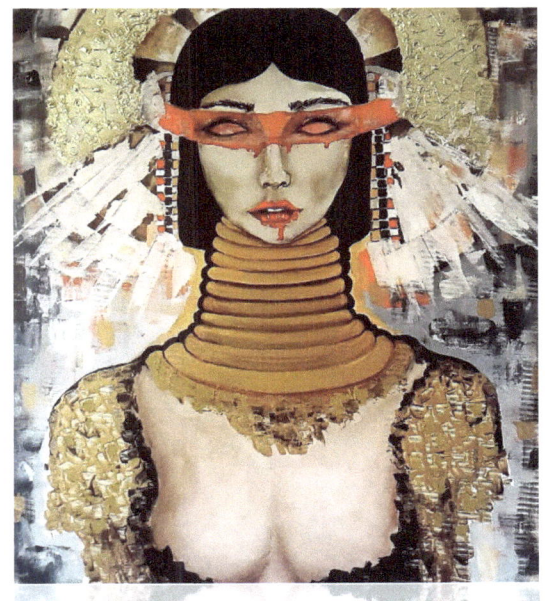

enhances the figure's striking features. This interplay between the abstract and the realistic elements encourages viewers to explore the painting more deeply, uncovering new details with each glance.

The artist's skillful blending of realism and abstraction results in a unique and captivating visual experience.

The detailed rendering of the figure's features, such as the delicate eyelashes and the subtle shading around the eyes, showcases the artist's meticulous attention to detail. Meanwhile, the fluid, abstract background elements add a layer of mystery and invite viewers to interpret the scene in their own way. This combination of styles creates a harmonious balance that is both visually engaging and thought-provoking.

The artist's intention behind "Ethereal Reverie" is to explore the duality of human existence—the outer calm and the inner complexity. By juxtaposing a serene, detailed portrait with an abstract, dynamic background, the artist aims to convey the contrast between our external appearances and the rich, often tumultuous inner worlds we carry within us. The closed eyes of the figure symbolize a retreat into one's thoughts, a moment of introspection where the boundaries between reality and imagination blur. Through this piece, the artist invites viewers to reflect on their own inner landscapes, encouraging a deeper understanding of the self and the myriad emotions that shape our experiences.

Well, "Ethereal Reverie" is a powerful piece that resonates on multiple levels. It invites viewers to pause and reflect, to consider the inner world of the subject, and to appreciate the harmonious interplay between realism and abstraction. The painting's rich textures and vibrant colors make it a visually engaging piece that captures the viewer's attention, while its emotional depth and symbolic richness offer a profound commentary on the human condition.

This artwork stands out not only for its aesthetic appeal but also for its ability to evoke a sense of calm and contemplation in those who view it.

4|Veil of Dreams

In this captivating work of art, the central figure exudes a serene grace, her visage partially obscured by a delicate blindfold that flows like silk across her eyes. This intentional concealment of sight invites the viewer to explore the concept of inner vision, urging us to look beyond the physical and delve into the realms of intuition and imagination. The golden hues that envelop her form are not merely decorative but serve as a radiant halo, imbuing

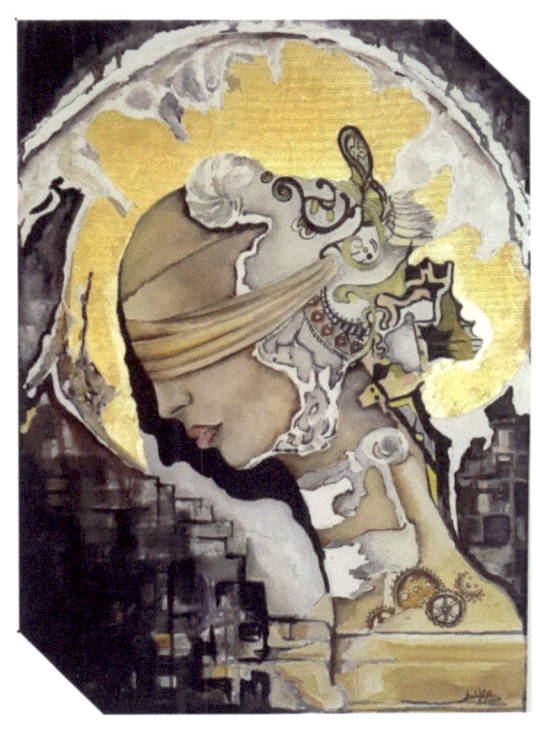

her with an ethereal aura that transcends the ordinary and touches upon the divine. Her gentle profile is adorned with intricate swirls and gears, an enigmatic blend of nature and machinery, symbolizing the harmony between the organic and the mechanical, the past and the future.

The background of this composition is a tapestry of contrasts, where shadowy architectural forms dissolve into abstract shapes, hinting at a cityscape that is both familiar and fantastical. The muted tones of gray and black provide a stark yet harmonious backdrop to the luminous gold, creating a visual symphony that dances between light and shadow. This interplay evokes a sense of mystery, drawing the viewer into a world where reality and imagination intertwine. The abstract forms invite endless interpretation, suggesting a landscape that shifts and morphs with each glance, a reflection of the ever-changing nature of perception and the fluidity of dreams.

Delicate brushstrokes craft the figure's features with exquisite precision, capturing the essence of tranquility and introspection.

"Veil of Dreams" is a mesmerizing exploration of duality and transformation. It invites the observer to ponder the balance between the seen and unseen, the tangible and the ethereal. This artwork is a poetic narrative, a visual meditation that resonates with the soul, urging one to embrace the beauty of the unknown and the endless possibilities that lie within the realms of imagination. It challenges us to question our perceptions, to seek beauty in complexity, and to find harmony in the interplay of contrasting elements. As we gaze upon this piece, we are reminded of the profound connection between art and the human experience, a connection that transcends time and space, uniting us in a shared journey of discovery and wonder.

5|Keys to the Soul

This striking artwork depicts a contemplative figure adorned with vibrant red curls, embodying a blend of strength and vulnerability. The figure's downcast gaze invites the viewer into a moment of introspection, suggesting a depth of thought and emotion. The warm, earthy tones create a comforting yet complex atmosphere, while the bold black and gold elements add a layer of intrigue. Each brushstroke seems to echo the nuances of the human experience, inviting an exploration of identity and self-discovery.

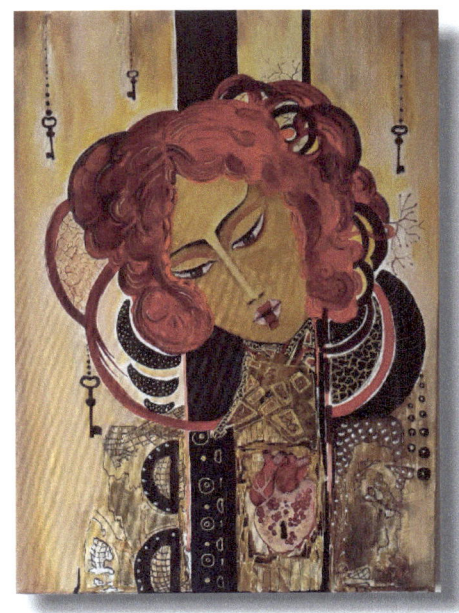

Suspended above the figure are keys, powerful symbols of access and revelation. These keys suggest the unlocking of hidden truths, representing the pathways to understanding oneself and others. They evoke the idea that within each of us lies the potential for growth, change, and enlightenment. This visual metaphor encourages viewers to consider the keys they possess in their own lives—the choices, experiences, and insights that shape their journeys.

The intricate patterns woven throughout the

composition serve to enrich the narrative, hinting at a complex tapestry of experiences that shape the figure's identity. The blending of textures and colors reflects the myriad emotions we encounter, from joy to sorrow, and highlights the beauty found within these contrasts. This artwork speaks to the universal human experience, inviting us to embrace our multifaceted nature.

At the heart of the piece is a striking representation of a heart, symbolizing both fragility and resilience. This central motif serves as a poignant reminder that our emotional core is both delicate and strong, capable of enduring life's challenges.

"Keys to the Soul" ultimately invites viewers to reflect on their own journeys, the secrets they hold, and the keys they possess to unlock deeper understanding and connection within themselves and the world around them.

6|Embrace Behind Bars

This captivating artwork features two figures locked in a tender embrace, highlighting the intimacy of their connection. The woman, adorned in golden hues, appears serene as she leans into her partner's kiss. Her vibrant red lips stand out, drawing the viewer's attention to the emotional depth of the moment. The man's presence is soft yet powerful, creating a sense of balance in their union.

The background is marked by bold vertical lines that resemble bars, introducing a layer of complexity to the scene. These lines suggest confinement or barriers, contrasting sharply with the freedom expressed in the couple's embrace. This duality invites viewers to reflect on the nature of love and the challenges that often accompany it. Despite the restrictions symbolized by the bars, the figures convey a powerful sense of connection.

Golden accents throughout the artwork enhance the richness of the scene. They symbolize warmth, passion, and the preciousness of love. The intricate detailing on the woman's attire adds a touch of elegance, while the patterns on her partner's skin evoke a sense of history and identity. Together, these elements create a visual harmony that captivates the eye.

The interplay of light and shadow adds depth to the composition, emphasizing the emotional weight of the moment. The gentle curves of the figures contrast with the sharp lines of the background, reinforcing the idea of love existing even in

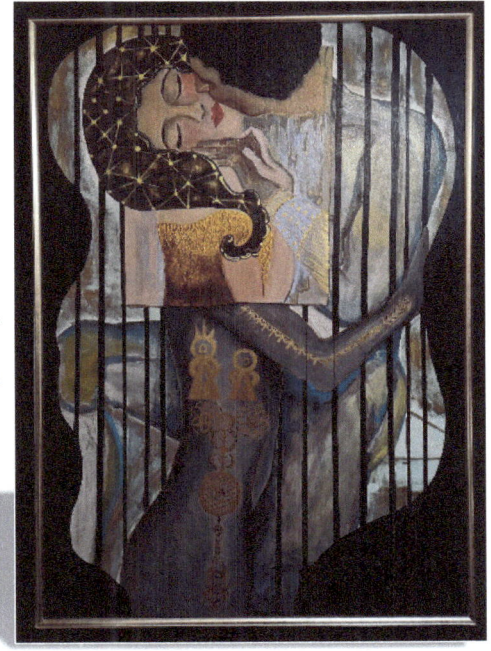

difficult circumstances. This artwork serves as a reminder that true connection can flourish despite external challenges.

Ultimately,"Embrace Behind Bars" invites viewers to ponder the complexities of love and intimacy. It speaks to the strength found in vulnerability and the beauty that emerges when two souls come together, even when faced with obstacles. This piece encourages us to celebrate the moments of closeness that transcend barriers, reminding us of the

enduring power of love.
7|Harmony of Life and Death

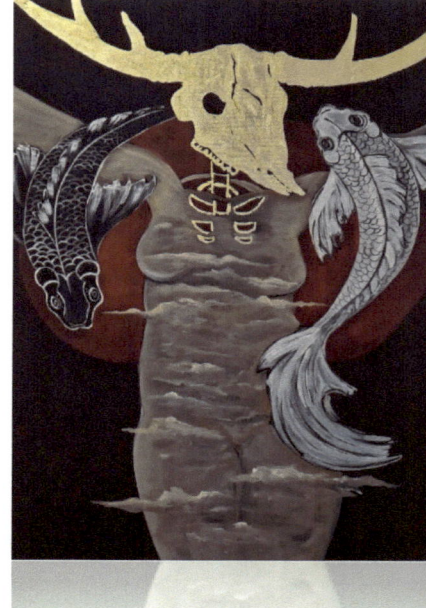

In this captivating artwork, the viewer is immediately drawn into a dialogue between life and death, masterfully illustrated through its striking imagery. At the heart of the composition lies a skeletal figure, crowned with a majestic deer skull, its golden accents shimmering against a dark, enigmatic background. This juxtaposition sets the stage for a profound exploration of existence, inviting contemplation on the transient nature of life.

Flanking the skeletal figure are two gracefully rendered koi fish, gliding effortlessly through the air. Their fluid movements symbolize resilience and transformation, embodying the spirit of life that persists even in the face of mortality. The use of monochromatic tones for the fish contrasts sharply with the vibrant red circle behind them, representing the sun or a new beginning. This interplay of colors serves to highlight the cycle of life, where every ending gives way to a new start.

The skeletal structure, intricately detailed with golden elements, suggests a reverence for the past and the wisdom that comes with it. The bones are not merely remnants of what once was; they are a testament to the journey of life. The artist's choice to incorporate skeletal imagery invites viewers to reflect on their own mortality and the legacies they leave behind.

Clouds drift softly around the figure, adding an ethereal quality to the composition. This element of the artwork evokes a sense of the sublime, bridging the earthly with the celestial. The clouds serve as a reminder of the ephemeral nature of life, hinting at the idea that existence is as fleeting as the wisps of mist that vanish into the air.

In conclusion, "Harmony of Life and Death" serves as a compelling reflection on the cyclical nature of existence. It encourages viewers to embrace life's fleeting moments while acknowledging the inevitability of death. Through its rich symbolism and masterful execution, this artwork challenges us to find beauty in both the transient and the eternal, reminding us that every experience contributes to the intricate tapestry of our being.

8| Dance of Light and Shadow

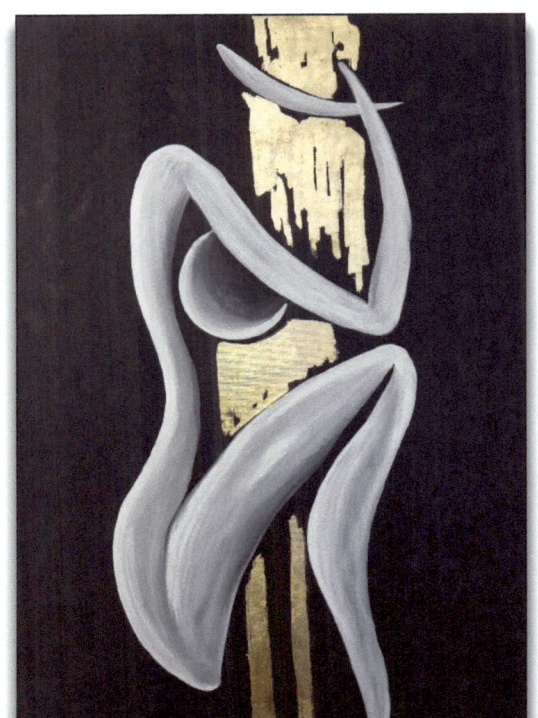

This artwork captures a unique blend of elegance and simplicity, inviting viewers into a world of movement and emotion.

The central figure, painted in soft gray tones, showcases smooth lines and gentle curves that evoke a sense of grace. Its pose seems to dance against the deep black background, creating a striking visual contrast that draws the eye.

The use of gray gives the figure a sense of calmness, while the black backdrop adds depth and mystery. This combination allows the viewer to focus on the fluidity of the figure, as it appears to be in motion. The artist's choice of colors creates an atmosphere that feels both serene and dynamic, encouraging contemplation.

Adding to the allure are the golden accents that break through the dark space. These shimmering elements resemble flowing ribbons of light, infusing the piece with joy and warmth. The gold not only highlights the figure but also symbolizes energy and vitality, making the artwork feel alive and vibrant.

The interplay of light and shadow in this piece adds another layer of meaning. The gray figure stands out boldly against the dark background, while the gold accents create a sense of illumination. This contrast speaks to the balance between darkness and light, a theme that resonates with many aspects of life.

Overall, this artwork is a celebration of beauty in movement and the harmony of contrasting elements. It invites viewers to reflect on their own experiences and emotions, making it a truly unique piece that resonates with everyone. Its simplicity and elegance make it accessible, allowing for a personal connection that lingers long after viewing.

9|Essence of Strength

In this striking artwork, the artist presents a powerful exploration of the human form, focusing on the essence of strength and vulnerability. The muscular figure, depicted without a head, symbolizes both physical prowess and the idea of identity stripped down to its core. The bold, monochromatic tones of gray emphasize the sculptural quality of the body, creating an immediate impact that draws the viewer in.

The choice of a dark background contrasts dramatically with the light gray of the figure, highlighting its muscular contours. This stark dichotomy invites contemplation on the nature of strength itself—how it can be both a source of pride and a mask for deeper emotions. The absence of a head suggests a departure from the traditional representation of self, prompting viewers to reflect on what it means to be strong in today's world.

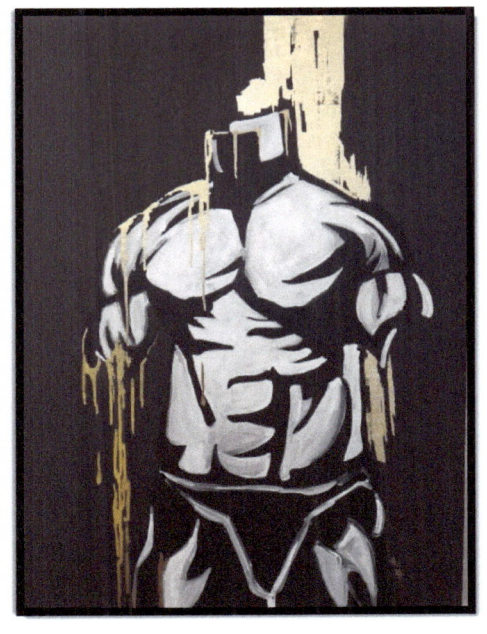

Golden drips cascade down the figure, adding a layer of richness and complexity. This shimmering element not only catches the eye but also acts as a metaphor for the struggles and triumphs that shape us. The gold represents resilience, reminding us that beauty can emerge from challenges. It transforms the raw power of the figure into something transcendent, suggesting that strength is not merely physical but also deeply emotional.

The interplay of light and dark throughout the piece serves to enhance the overall theme. The shadows evoke a sense of mystery, while the gold accents illuminate the figure's form, creating a dance between visibility and obscurity. This dynamic invites viewers to engage with the artwork on multiple levels, encouraging them to consider their own experiences with strength and self-identity.

Ultimately, "Essence of Strength" is a thought-provoking piece that challenges conventional ideas of masculinity and power. It encourages a deeper understanding of what it means to be human, celebrating both the physical and emotional aspects of our existence. Through its unique composition and bold use of color, this artwork resonates with anyone who has ever grappled with their own sense of identity and strength.

10|Embrace of Unity

This captivating artwork beautifully depicts two figures entwined in a tender embrace, symbolizing connection and togetherness. The figures are rendered in deep black, creating a powerful backdrop that emphasizes their forms. The artist's choice of colors creates a striking contrast that draws the viewer's attention, inviting them to explore the emotional depth of the piece.

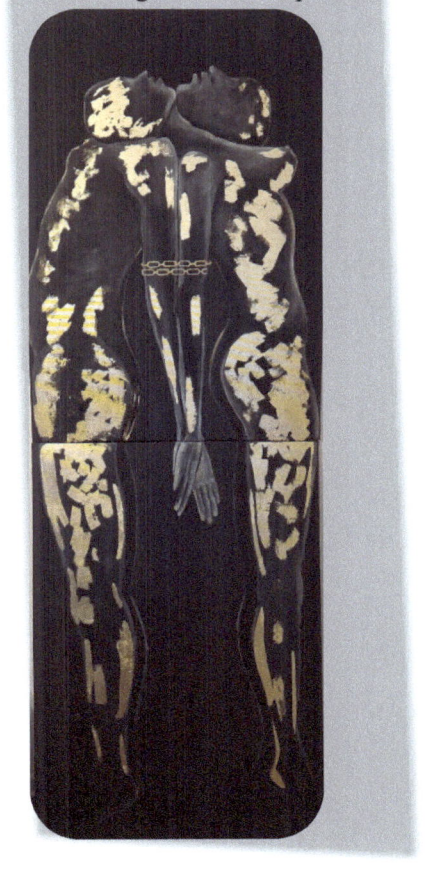

The figures face each other, their heads tilted back in a serene pose. This positioning suggests a moment of vulnerability and intimacy, capturing the essence of a close bond. The smooth lines of their bodies flow seamlessly into one another, illustrating the idea that love and connection transcend individuality. The simplicity of their forms allows the viewer to focus on the emotion conveyed through their posture.

Golden accents adorn the figures, adding a layer of richness and warmth to the artwork. These shimmering details appear like patches of light, symbolizing hope and strength within their unity.

The gold highlights not only enhance the visual appeal but also serve as a reminder of the beauty found in relationships. They reflect the idea that love can illuminate even the darkest of moments.The arms of the figures intertwine, with one hand reaching out to connect with the other. This gesture signifies support and trust, essential elements in any relationship. The delicate positioning of their hands suggests that even in stillness, there is movement—a dynamic energy that flows between them. The artist captures the essence of companionship, reminding us of the importance of connection in our lives.

Overall, "Embrace of Unity" is a powerful exploration of love and togetherness. Through its bold use of color and form, the artwork encourages viewers to reflect on their own relationships and the bonds they share. It celebrates the beauty of connection, inviting us to cherish the moments of intimacy that define our existence.

11|Whispers of Emotion

This artwork stands out as a profound exploration of human emotion, captured through the graceful portrayal of a woman's face amidst flowing hair. The use of black and white emphasizes the stark contrast between light and shadow, drawing the viewer into a world of introspection. The simplicity of the color palette allows the intricate details of the figure to shine, creating a unique visual experience.

The woman's expression is serene yet powerful, embodying a sense of calm and strength. Her closed eyes and slightly parted lips suggest a moment of deep reflection, inviting viewers to connect with their own feelings. The flowing lines of her hair echo the fluidity of thought and emotion, illustrating how our inner experiences can be both beautiful and complex. This connection between the figure and her flowing hair serves as a metaphor for the intertwining of thoughts and feelings.Golden drips cascade from the top of the canvas, adding an element of richness and warmth to the piece. These golden accents represent moments of clarity and insight that can emerge from the depths of our emotions. The shimmering quality of the gold contrasts beautifully with the dark background, symbolizing hope and enlightenment

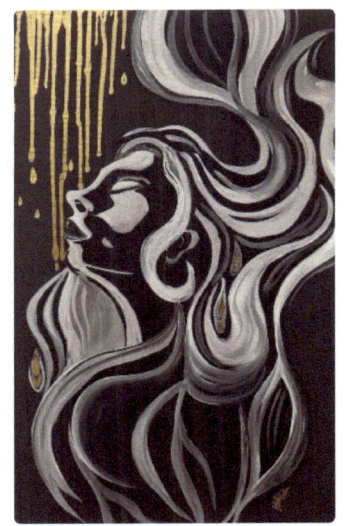

amidst the chaos of life. This interplay of colors creates a dynamic visual rhythm that keeps the viewer engaged.

The artist's choice to focus on the woman's face while allowing her hair to dominate the composition speaks to the themes of identity and self-expression. It highlights the idea that our emotions are an integral part of who we are, shaping our perceptions and interactions with the world. The flowing hair serves as a reminder that our thoughts and feelings can be as fluid as water, constantly shifting and evolving.In "Whispers of Emotion," the artist masterfully captures the complexity of human experience. Through the interplay of color, expression, and form, this artwork invites viewers to reflect on their own emotions and the beauty found within them. It stands as a testament to the power of art to evoke feelings and provoke thought, making it a truly unique piece worthy of contemplation.

ABOUT THE ARTIST

Jiji Madalina, a remarkable artist hailing from the heart of Romania, weaves her rich cultural heritage into every piece she creates. With a passion for art that transcends boundaries, Jiji draws inspiration from the vibrant landscapes and storied traditions of her homeland. Her unique perspective allows her to blend the old with the new, creating works that resonate deeply with viewers and invite them into her world.

Each image showcased in this book is a testament to Jiji's exceptional talent and commitment to her craft. The pages come alive with color and emotion, reflecting her journey as an artist. Every brushstroke tells a story, embodying the essence of her experiences and the beauty she finds in everyday life. It is an invitation to explore not just her art, but the profound connection between creativity and personal expression.

For those captivated by Jiji's work, all the pieces featured in this book are available for sale. If you wish to acquire a piece that speaks to you, please reach out via email at georgianajijie@gmail.com. Jiji Madalina's art is not just a visual experience; it is an opportunity to own a piece of her artistic journey and to bring a touch of Romania's spirit into your own life.

www.ingramcontent.com/pod-product-compliance
Lightning Source LLC
Chambersburg PA
CBHW040349220526
45473CB00009B/2821